I have had the pleasure of reading this book before printing. It is a must for all levels of agents. It is a practical, innovative, and *current* guide to success!

—Mike Brodie of Keller Williams, Plano, TX
Operating Partner and Broker/Owner

In this book, Glenn provides an easy step-by-step guide on the actions and mindshare needed to dominate and succeed in the "new normal." This is a great read from someone who has years of experience!

—Terri Spilsbury, Keller Williams ELITE Realty,
Owner/Operating Principal/Managing Broker

I just loved it! It was like a deep breath of fresh, cold, mountain air!

Everyone is talking about the new normal, but nobody was prepared to take on the new challenge. So, here it is. What are you going to do with it? Roll up your sleeves, and follow the eight steps—nothing more, nothing less.

Thank you, Glenn, for laying out this roadmap for us as a reminder that we all face the same challenges around the world.

—Ilena Preda KW, Top Agent,
Bucharest, Romania

Shutdown Slingshot strikes the right balance between providing inspirational perspective and practical and actionable advice on how real estate teams, agents, and brokers can set up for sustained and significant success in their real estate careers. This 100-day playbook is a must-read for anyone in the real-estate industry who is looking to level-up in a post-COVID world.

—Lauren Haw CEO & Broker of Record,
Zoocasa Realty Inc., Brokerage

Glenn McQueenie does it again with his book *Shutdown Slingshot*! As Glenn writes, "with every change comes great opportunity," and he nicely shows real estate agents how to capitalize on this new reality. This book will serve agents for years to come, as it is truly not just about adjusting to the new 2020 pandemic reality. Rather, Glenn presents a combination of the tried and true, capably mixed in with the real estate industry's new reality, or what Glenn aptly calls "digital/virtual reality." Forget the references to any dates, as this book will serve real estate agents for many years beyond 2020. This book is written for any real estate agent who truly wants to call their careers a business.

—Anne St Dennis, Co-fondateur/Operating
Partner, KW URBAIN, Montréal, Québec, Canada
Co-fondateur/Controlling Partner,
KW MOMENTUM, Brossard, Québec, Canada
Controlling Partner, KW CONNEXION, Montréal,
Québec, Canada
Founding Partner, KW ROMANIA, Romania, Europe
KW Worldwide Accredited Faculty Trainer

Glenn's new book is a must-read if you are in the middle of a pandemic or you just want to relaunch your production. Glenn has lived his life in such a way to be the perfect leader for any serious real estate agent who wants to build a successful real estate business. It's filled with practical action steps to ensure your success, so read and then reread this book every year of your career until you have the success you deserve! Personally, having over 30 plus years in the real estate business with consistently selling over 200 plus homes each year, I know great advice when I read it!

—Linda Mckissack, podcast host of *Everything Life and Real Estate*, author of *Presentation Mastery for Realtors* and the bestseller, *Hold, How to Find Buy and Rent Homes to Build Wealth*

Glenn slingshots you through the next five to ten years of our rapidly changing real estate business in less than an hour. I thought I was doing well during this break in my business, but Glenn made me realize there's so much more to do. This book can lift you up from any stage in your business and help you see the next level. I loved every minute of it, and I know you will, too.

—Chuck Charlton, Team Leader & Eight-Time Top 100 agent in Canada, Royal LePage

Shutdown Slingshot

Eight Winning Mindsets Real Estate Agents Need to Double-Down over the Next 100 Days

GLENN MCQUEENIE

AUTHOR ACADEMY

Printed in the United States of America

Published by Author Academy Elite
PO Box 43, Powell, OH 43065
www.AuthorAcademyElite.com

Identifiers:

LCCN: 2020909610

ISBN: 978-1-64746-297-0 (paperback)
ISBN: 978-1-64746-298-7 (hardback)
ISBN: 978-1-64746-299-4 (ebook)

Available in paperback, hardback, e-book, and audiobook

Any Internet addresses (websites, blogs, etc.) and telephone numbers printed in this book are offered as a resource. They are not intended in any way to be or imply an endorsement by Author Academy Elite, nor does Author Academy Elite vouch for the content of these sites and numbers for the life of this book.

Book design by JetLaunch. Cover design by Debbie O'Byrne.

Dedication

To the great real estate agents who safely guide their clients through complex transactions by adding value and confidence every step of the way.

TABLE OF CONTENTS

FOREWORD

Throughout history, people have battled obstacles of fear and doubt during everyday life.

This time, it is different. During the COVID-19 pandemic, we have seen an outcry of fear raging across the globe. Social media and digital devices have brought this crisis closer to home. We have witnessed a planet-wide shutdown—physically, mentally, emotionally, and financially. People are stuck and scared.

It is no different in the real estate industry.

Thankfully, my friend Glenn McQueenie, entrepreneur, owner of multiple real estate brokerages with Keller Williams, and a faculty instructor at Keller Williams University, teaches us a way forward. He created a relevant roadmap showing us how to turn obstacles into opportunities. In it, he encourages real estate agents to leverage the shut down as a time to double down. Now is the best time for real estate agents to serve their clients at the highest level and gain massive market share.

In this book, you'll discover eight winning mindsets to gain confidence, clarity, and insight. Glenn's writing is direct and to the point. This book may be small, but it is packed with everything an agent needs to stack the odds in their favor and ensure their business does not go under now or in the future.

As a licensed realtor for over thirty years, Glenn knows how to generate victory in favorable and unfavorable economies alike. The insight he has into real estate is second to none. His passion is contagious. He's committed to equipping leaders and entrepreneurs to fortify their minds, double down, and operate successfully during the pandemic and beyond.

Get ready to make your next 100 days your best days yet.

—Kary Oberbrunner, author of *Day Job to Dream Job,*
Elixir Project, Unhackable

PREFACE

In the middle of March 2020, the game changed. The news reported COVID-19, a highly contagious virus, was spreading around the world. Governments responded immediately by shutting down their borders and economies. Suddenly, we started to understand that we really do not have control over many things. Our mobility, recreation, workplace, dining experiences, and most social activities were gone, all in the name of social distancing and flattening the curve.

I wrote this book as a wake-up call to the real estate industry. During the first eight weeks of the pandemic shutdown, I spoke to hundreds of agents to check in and see how they were holding up. Broadly speaking, their responses fell into three categories. 20% were in full lie-down (shutdown) mode, choosing to cease all business until they received the all-clear signal. Another 20% went into double-down mode, reaching out to their clients and checking–in to see how they were doing. The remaining 60% had no idea what to do or even which way they were leaning.

I realized this was primarily a mindset issue.

What follows is a story on how to embrace the eight winning mindsets to get your unfair share of the market. I hope this inspires you to get out of lie-down mode and into double-down mode. Every shift in the market can be viewed as a negative or a positive. If you choose this as a positive and seize the opportunity that a shift creates, you will build an amazing real estate business. There has never been a better time in my thirty-one years in the industry for you to have the opportunity to build market share. While others yearn for the good ole days, you seize the opportunity and adopt the eight winning mindsets of the 100-day sprint that will follow this shutdown.

INTRODUCTION

The purpose of this book is to provide a wake-up call and roadmap for not only our 570 amazing associates but also to other real estate agents at their respective companies. I believe the work you do now will set you up for the final two quarters of 2020 and the rest of your real estate career.

Additionally, my other goal is to provide a new way of thinking about what it takes to win the *new game* of real estate. What is the new road map for us to follow in the post-pandemic period?

<u>What is the biggest difference it will make?</u>

The agents who use this book over the next 100 days (starting first within the next thirty days) will take a massive market share from those who have shut down and cease to work during the pandemic. While some agents shut down,

I want you to double-down. Doubling-down will increase business and allow you to avoid database shrinkage through loss to your competition, and it will prepare you for a quick recovery in the post-pandemic world. The seeds we sow now will be harvested in the fall.

This is your time to get a head-start on your competition. While many realtors will waste their time getting caught up on Netflix, you will spend your time learning, building new systems, adding new tools, and increasing your capabilities.

A shift in the market gives you a once-in-a-lifetime opportunity to build your brand, gain mindshare, and take market share from your competitors. You can move your business ahead three years in the next 100 days! Think about it—when will you ever have an opportunity like this again?

What does your business look like 100 days from now?

It is faster, simpler, easier, more systematic, and predictable. You have shifted to the new digital/virtual experience and away from having to be physically in your office or with your clients. You are doing ten virtual listing presentations per day. You are doing buyer consultations on one of the many digital platforms, and your showings are now 80% virtual (along with your open houses). You are no longer driving back and forth across the city, and you spend your time in your top 20% activities that generate the highest return. Your costs are going down, and you can work anywhere you choose. Most importantly, you no longer work the sixty to eighty hours per week.

By doing the 100-day sprint, you become the *hunter* instead of the one being hunted. Many of the pre-pandemic disruptors like Opendoor, Offerpad, Redfin, and Zillow have laid off their staff, delayed/bailed on their Ibuyer direct home purchases, and are desperately trying to figure out what their next steps are to survive.

They believed they could reduce us to salaried salespeople. They thought that Real Estate was a simple commodity business, like the travel industry. They thought they could digitize 95% of the transaction and pocket the fees we make by getting rid of agents. They raised billions in capital markets and now realize that real estate is a business centered on people, not on an algorithm.

Agents that have been around for a long time realize these simple truths:

1. Every transaction is 90% emotional and 10% transactional.

2. Logic makes people think, but emotions make people act.

3. Their success in real estate is 90% mindset and 10% skills.

4. The agents who receive the most repeat business and referrals from their sphere of influence and past clients also give back to those people at a very high level. They give to get.

This book will focus on the eight winning mindsets you need to survive and thrive in the post-pandemic world:

1. Digitize everything you do, and act virtually.

2. Be disruptive. Be really disruptive.

3. Be learning-based and open to the opportunity.

4. Be a game-changer.

5. Focus on results—it's progress, not perfection.

6. Always be working on your inner game to have the best outer game.

7. Be driven to grow, and have a growth mindset.

8. Constantly test the market. Get feedback from the market and adapt.

Things seemed to be going pretty well for most people in the first quarter of 2020. During that time, we slowly started to hear about a virus that originated in Wuhan, China. Nearing the mid-point of March, governments around the world began to announce a new thing called "shelter-in-place." At first, they told us the shelter-in-place would last two weeks, which then led to a month. Then, they added another month, maybe two, and said it will probably be eighteen months to get back to the level of freedom we had before the pandemic.

The game changed. Suddenly, we realized all of the things we thought we were in control of could be taken away in a second. We began to understand that we do not really have control over many things. Our mobility, recreation, workplace, dining experiences, and most social activities were gone, all in the name of social distancing.

But the one thing they cannot take away is your choice of what to do in these scary-times.

You have four choices:

1. Panic.

2. Freeze up and take no action.

3. Be too optimistic and deny reality.

4. Be practical, pragmatic, opportunistic, proactive, and positive.

I love the following quotes below:

❖ *Life is about circumstances, opportunities and outcomes. 2020 will dictate your available opportunities, but it will not determine your outcome...you do!*

—Author unknown

❖ *Whatever you think you can, or think you can't, you are right.*

—Henry Ford

❖ *Destiny is not a matter of chance, it is a matter of choice, it is not a thing to be waited for, it is a thing to be achieved.*

—William Jennings Bryant

The choice is up to you. You can go into panic-mode and make some really bad decisions. You can freeze and be non-active and stay on the sidelines. You can let the pandemic/shutdown define you and change the trajectory of your life. You can let it destroy you and everything you have, and if you do, it will take a long time for you to recover. Or, let this be a source of strength and inspiration. I encourage you to be practical, pragmatic, opportunistic, proactive, and positive. I hope you choose the latter.

This is our time to start our 100-day sprint and win our unfair share of the market. What you do in the next thirty, sixty, ninety, and 100 days will determine your last two quarters of 2020! It makes no sense to panic and freeze or to be too optimistic and deny the new realities that we face. The only way to win this game is to be practical, pragmatic, and extremely opportunistic!

100-day Sprint Goals:

1. Get you and your business back into gear for 2020.

2. Continue your shift to virtual/digital platforms before a new disruptor enters the marketplace.

3. Stop being a *secret agent,* and let people know what you are up to.

4. Fill your pipeline with ready buyers/listings as the marketplace re-opens.

5. Complete the migration or understanding of the tools of the trade.

6. Achieve 100% understanding of the eight mindsets and how to run your new playbook.

7. Get into action by following steps at the end of each chapter

Use the next 100 days of 2020 and the coming quarters to achieve 100% of your potential. Bring 100% of your vitality, passion, joy, and presence to the goals that you set for yourself. Think about what it takes to *go all in* for you. Think about what it takes to elevate your purpose, life, and business satisfaction each day. It is time for your 100-day sprint!

1
DIGITIZER

Go digital and virtual as soon as possible

WHAT DOES YOUR digital business look like 100 days from now? While your competition watches Netflix, you gain the once-in-a-lifetime opportunity to build your brand, gain mindshare (which builds market share later), and move your business ahead one-two years in the next 100 days.

Your business is easier, faster, simpler, more systematic, and predictable. You have shifted to a virtual/physical experience for your clients, and you are on your way to making it an almost 80/20 split.

This begins with you focusing on all of the new digital capabilities that we have today. What a great tool Zoom Video or other platforms are, which give us an incredible opportunity to broadcast content, host how-to seminars, or do as many listing/buying consultations as possible.

Imagine that instead of driving an hour to and from an appointment, you can simply schedule an initial consultation for thirty minutes. You could do ten of these per day! We can now show 80% of the homes virtually, via 3D or virtual tours. We also have Seller/Listing Agent guided tours!

We have professionally guided virtual open houses available by appointment. The race is on to make all steps of the home buying/selling process as digital/virtual as possible. You win the race when all of your systems and support material make the entire process an amazing experience for your consumer.

In addition to YouTube educational videos/seminars and infographics on every step of the transaction, you can create virtual home inspections and even virtual closings.

You are learning how to run digital ads via Facebook, Linked-in, Instagram, Youtube, Google, etc. Which ads convert? Which do not? What are the best practices around this? Do I leverage this entire area to someone else?

The choices you make will define the future trajectory of your business. The wrong choice could destroy you and everything you have. The right choice can be a tremendous source of strength and inspiration as you continue to take market share from your competition.

Diagnose your current state of thinking, then commit to making the required changes to get to a whole new level of success. Choose to go digital/virtual and become a *hunter* for the next 100 days. Set your goals and do the work. Set your plan because you said you would!

Before we jump into the book, take a self-assessment, and get really clear where you are right now.

Survival mode: Zero to eight deals per year.

- Action: Moving from survival to stability requires you to change your daily habits and action. It is about a transition from living in a world that makes you feel frustrated most of the time and looking for who is to blame (your spouse, colleagues, office, broker, all buyers and sellers), to a world where you change first before expecting the world to change for you. When you change the way you look at things, the things you look at change.

<u>Stability:</u> Ten to twenty-five deals per year.

- Action: This is where you change your thinking to solve problems.

- To move from stability to success requires you to change your thinking. We change our thinking by receiving great mentoring and coaching from those who are more successful.

- You also focus this time on reading and learning—all of the things you previously told yourself you do not have time for. You do—there is a pandemic.

- Through new habits, activities, and systems, you get your business stabilized. Now is the time to get moving toward success.

<u>Success:</u> Twenty-five to fifty deals per year.

- To be successful requires you to take the focus off of yourself and put it onto others. You also start to add leverage of other people into your business. In my experience, most agents can handle thirty-five transactions by themselves before getting maxed out. Your first key hire should be an administrative assistant, either full or part-time. They will take away everything that is not in your top 20%, such as paperwork, compliance, building, and running your database, etc.

- Ask yourself:

    i. How can I help my client achieve what they want?

    ii. How can I systemize my business so that we can prevent unnecessary errors and deliver a world-class experience?

    iii. How do I become more virtual and less physical?

Transition from success to significance: Fifty-plus deals per year.

- Action: This is the big jump from transactional to transformational. It is about changing lives, not just getting another deal. There is complete removal of any focus on yourself and replacing it with: *How can I impact my clients and the community?* You become a community leader and also the leader of your growing real estate team. You start asking these questions:

    i. How can our team provide the ultimate experience for clients?

    ii. How can I help everyone get what they want so I can get what I want?

    iii. What unique solution do I provide to create a unique experience and build a tribe of raving fans?

    iv. Do I have the right people in all of the right positions on my team?

It does not matter what level you are at today. Every level begins with focusing on relationship first—deals/transactions will follow. Do not *fear your sphere of influence.* The lowest hanging fruit is the people you already have a relationship with and know and trust you. These are ten times easier to deal with than cold prospects who do not like, trust, or know you. This is the time you gain mindshare now, and market share later.

All change begins by telling yourself the truth first. Where are you now, and where do you want to go?

This 100-day sprint is about getting into alignment with your clients and focusing on getting them what they want, and then you get what you want. Life is about circumstances, opportunities, and outcomes. When you make the digital/virtual leap, you will see the gift of all of the available opportunities.

Finally, stay focused and set clear boundaries with your family, friends, and clients during the 100-day sprint. Start installing the systems and people into your business to make it more predictable, stable, simpler, easier, and more enjoyable for your customer. All change begins by telling yourself the truth first. Where are you today and where do you want to go? Do you want to stay in Shutdown mode, and just lie down and take what this market gives you? Or do you want to *double down* and get your unfair share of the market? The box below illustrates the difference between the two mindsets.

Digitizer	
Lie down	Double down
Freeze up and take no action.	Double their efforts on Lead generation
Digital is overrated	Digital/Virtual agents win the game
Physical marketing materials	Digital ads through Facebook, Instagram
No mentor or coach	Has multiple mentors and coaches
Physical appointments	Digital appointments
Zoom what?	Zoom trainings, showings, offers
Counts deals	Counts relationships

Action steps:

1. For the first thirty days, try to get to 50% virtual, 50% physical deliverable in your business.

2. Begin your mastery of Zoom by focusing on basics such as background, and be centered on camera. Consultations have a beginning, middle, end, and a call to action.

3. Speed up implementation of everything virtually, including consultations, showings, open houses, and step-by-step guides.

4. Diagnose your current thinking.

5. Learn as much as you can about digital marketing through Facebook, Instagram, Linked-in, YouTube, and Google

6. Be honest with yourself about where you are right now in your production, and commit to moving to the next level.

7. Focus on relationships first, and the deals will follow. Check-in on all your active and passive clients and ask, "How are you holding up?"

2
DISRUPTER

Make every step of the real estate transaction easier for the consumer, and take your unfair share of the market.

THE NEXT MINDSET we have to adopt is that of being incredibly disruptive. In the marketplace, you will either be the disrupter or the one being disrupted. You are either going to be the hunter or the one being hunted. I am telling you right now—I would rather be the hunter than be the hunted. Now is the time for us to get proactive and disrupt the market instead of being reactive and dealing with whatever happens out in the marketplace.

So, for some of you right now, your mindset is not about being disruptive. You feel so bogged down right now with all the complexity and the unpredictable changes in the marketplace, and you want to bury your head in the sand and hope it goes away. You do not know how long this pandemic will last, and you will probably ask yourself how much longer you want to be in this business. Am I really going to last? That is not the winning mindset to have about being disruptive.

I think the best mindset about being disruptive is stating that you understand this is a new game right now. And the beautiful thing about having a new game right now is that this is going to be the biggest transfer of market share that you are ever going to see in your career. There has never been a time when the market has been paused for two-three months. This will end up putting a lot of your competitive agents and brokerages out of business.

I remember when I first started in 1989 as the new kid on the block entering into my first brokerage, and things were going really well in Toronto. That year was another record as prices went up 20 or 30%. Most of the agents in the office were doing very well. And when everyone was doing well, I found it really hard to get market share from the agents who had been in business for a long time. So, I kept working away.

Then, there was the 1990 market crash.

The five-year mortgage rate was 14.25%. A $300,000 mortgage carried for $3,600/month. Today, a monthly mortgage payment of $3,600 would carry a mortgage of $790,000.

The sales volume dropped about 70%, and prices declined by about 40% over the next couple of years. Most of the existing agents could not adapt and longed for the *good old days*.

They were biding their time, waiting for the market to go back to where it was before it crashed.

I did not really know much of what the *good* market was like before, because I was so new in the business. So, I kept working and lead generating and testing new approaches. I kept trying to think of new ways to get business. The old ways of doing business were not working anymore.

So, I guess in my own way, I was being disruptive very early in my career. It paid off for me because within three years, I became the number one agent out of 230 salespeople. More importantly, I watched as a bunch of the top real estate agents and brokerages refused to change. Offices that were in the top twenty brokerages in Toronto marketplace went under. Big names like NRS, Family Trust, and Countrywide disappeared. I also watched a lot of the top producers disappear. They were so leveraged, and they had a lot of nice homes, drove expensive cars, and had really beautiful spouses. I watched as the houses disappeared. Their Cadillac STS, which was the big car at the time, soon became the Ford Taurus, and then their spouses also seemed to disappear. And for many people, they never recovered because they liked the old way of doing business too much.

When I talk about being disruptive, I'm excited for you and the opportunity you get to disrupt the marketplace.

I believe the future belongs to real estate agents and brokers who can deliver better digital marketing and better customer service. The future belongs to the agents and brokers who, during this shut down, decide to race ahead of everyone else and *double down*. The new game is to use all of the current technology that exists, adapt quickly, and put it into your business as fast as possible. There is nothing new in webinars and 3D virtual tours, but there is a lot to innovate with virtual presentations, showings, and open houses.

There are many ways to play the game of real estate sales. If the tactics that worked in the past are no longer effective for you, change the game. It is time to innovate. Get really clear on the new marketplace, arm yourself with research and data, and learn scripts that address customer fears and needs. You are an experienced professional, a valued consultant, and a trusted advisor. In a shifted market, the consumer needs you more than ever. This is the time when the lower-skilled agents leave the business and the pros take-off. There is always a flight to quality in tough times. The goal is to learn the new game as quickly as possible.

The new game is to digitize every step of the real estate process and set up to make the transaction faster, simpler, and easier for the consumer.

1. Virtual Buyer/Seller Consultations

2. Virtual showings with homes virtually staged

3. Virtual open houses

4. All paperwork digitized and signed electronically

5. Offers accepted before seeing the home

6. Virtual home inspection

7. Virtual appraisals

8. Virtual financing

9. Planning the new décor is done virtually, prior to closing. All home décor, paint, and renovations that buyer was going to complete are staged virtually, prior to closing.

10. The thirty-days to closing process is digitized.

11. Lawyers close transaction without ever meeting client face-to-face

12. Rental properties are viewed virtually

The new game is digital and virtual. The faster you make every step of the real estate transaction easier for the consumer, the quicker you take your unfair share of the market. This begins with taking all of the existing digital capabilities that we have and stitching them together to create a world-class experience for the consumer.

Build your new model with all of the value that you are going to give to your clients, and do it at a price others cannot compete with.

Remember, you always want to be proactive, and never reactive.

Disrupter	
Lie Down	Double down
Is being disrupted	Is the disruptor
Sticks their head in the sand	Runs to the new possibilities of market
Loved the good ole days	Grateful for opportunity to gain m-share
Won't play new game	Understand it is a new game right now
Is being hunted	Is the hunter

Action steps:

1. Understand it is a new game right now.

2. This will be the biggest transfer of market share that you are ever going to see in your career.

3. While others shut down, decide to race ahead of everyone else and double down.

4. Every step of the real estate process is digitized.

5. Build your new model with all of the value that you are going to give to your clients, and do it at a price that others cannot compete with.

6. Be the hunter, not the hunted.

3
LEARNER

Adopt the mindset that everything you have learned is preparation for greater learning.

TO WIN THE 100-day sprint, you have got to be as learning-based as possible. Over the last twelve weeks in our offices, we have been doing an increased number of coaching, learning, and teaching sessions via Zoom. The content that we have been creating and what our agents have been consuming is off the charts. I really looked at the first six weeks, which paralleled the way most people look at the six stages of grieving: shock, denial, anger, depression, bargaining, and acceptance.

Once we got over the initial shock and denial of what quarantined meant in our lives, we moved into anger. Who took away control of my life? Why did they take away my way of living? How do they expect me to survive if I cannot leave my home and go to work? Gradually, people moved out of anger, through depression, and eventually moved into bargaining. They started reaching out to friends, past clients, active clients, etc. Through listening and sharing their stories, most of us have moved into acceptance.

Once we get to acceptance, we can settle down, accept the facts, and start creating a new future. This starts by doing what you need to do right now to win the 100-day sprint. Over the past nine weeks and for the next couple of weeks, this is the time to learn. When this whole thing is over, and the *all clear* signal goes on, that is the time that you get to earn!

Now you have a choice.

Some people have used the weeks to watch unusual amounts of television news, Netflix, or read fiction books. But to really get ahead and win this 100-day sprint, it is time to go!

The people who are going to win the next game and win the next market are going to be the people who use this time to learn. They take their knowledge and improve every tool they have. The new race in real estate is to get to 80-90% virtual and 10-20% physical. Sure, there will still be clients who want to see a million homes, but most of the marketplace is looking for a faster, simpler, and easier way to buy and sell a home. These are some of the realities you need to understand to win this 100-day sprint.

I think the worst mindset you can have is to feel that you already know everything you need to know, and you see no reason to waste any more time or effort on new learning. That is what we call the fixed mindset, which is not the mindset you need to win the 100-day sprint. The real winning mindset is that you see everything you have learned is preparation for greater learning. It is always trying to get better for the sake of getting better to grow your business. I am always improving all of my systems, tools, technology, presentations, and scripts. I review how I appear on Zoom. Is the camera positioned properly? Are my slides legible? Does my presentation have a beginning, middle, and end?

I am learning and improving on all of those skills right now to make sure I win this game. There are a lot of skills you need right now to win the virtual game. One of the skills you need to learn is how to do a virtual presentation. You have to learn how to smile. You must learn how to get your nerves under control and be able to present in front of a camera. What a gift that you can do a listing presentation in thirty minutes instead of taking three hours to drive and present.

How do you keep your energy high and have lots of fun? How can you learn to establish credibility with your audience right away and learn how to become a better presenter?

Learn to share your stories. Share your triumphs and also the mistakes you have made. The real goal here is to try to learn the skills you need to build and establish your credibility to build trust with our audience. You are going to have to learn the virtual game right now.

So, the most important thing is to learn and have focus. Focus on what you need to learn. Study the market like you have never studied before. Gain the knowledge to tell all the buyers what is going on in all the different price ranges. Is this market moving for first-time buyers? How does it look for the move-up or luxury market? Are the prices rising or declining these markets? What about sellers? Do you know the local market better than they do?

I have been at parties before when someone asks, "Hey, Glenn, what did that house sell for down the street?" Most of the time, I do not know because there are so many different markets. Many people think we know what every single property sells for. So, at every party, there is always a *Mary* who is not in real estate but knows more about the local market than I do. *Mary* jumps in and says what the property was listed for, but she heard there were eight offers. You just sit there and think, *Thanks, Mary.*

You have to brush up your knowledge on market trends and what is going on in the economy right now. What are the average days on market? What are the sales to ask ratios right now? What are the inventory levels? Are there a lot of power sales or distressed sales in the marketplace right now? How about brushing up on your emotional intelligence? Should you learn more about empathy and the ability to walk a mile in someone else's shoes? Is it learning how the mind works? Is it learning how to manage different people in different situations?

What are some of the habits that are serving you really well? And what habits have you been carrying for a long time which no longer serve your needs?

As far as being learning-based, you do not want to have the worst mindset, thinking you already know everything. You want to have the positive mindset and positive attitude that says everything you have ever learned so far has been a foundation and preparation for new learning. It is about learning for doing, not learning for knowing. Your friends who win all the trivia competitions know a lot about everything, but they do not know a whole lot about one thing. You get paid a whole lot of money to know about your one thing.

How great are your skills on getting the right listing price? We know 99% of marketing a home is basically the price, and if you get that wrong, it does not matter how well you virtually stage it, show it, do virtual open houses, or create the best virtual real estate system in the world. If you do not know how to price a property, then you are not going to sell. This is the game of being so learning-based right now that a brush up on our skills will allow us to win the 100-day sprint.

Go back to the basics: Gary Keller states in his book, *The Millionaire Real Estate Agent,* that real estate is all about three things: Leads, Listings, and Leverage.

<u>Leads:</u> Get real with yourself. Every one of you has the ability to handle an incoming lead from a customer who asks if they could sell their house or asks for help to buy one. But not everyone in our industry can initiate a lead. Are you a natural (or want to be a) lead generator? Or are you a lead receiver? This industry needs both types to operate effectively. We need the hunters and the skinners. If you love to lead generate, then you should be building a team. If you are a lead receiver, you should be on a team.

<u>Listings</u>

- Listings maximize your time and dollar per-hour compensation.

- Every listing could bring at least four more pieces of business. You can meet additional buyers, sellers, and neighbours that all have a real estate need.

- Listings create top of mind positioning in the neighbourhood.

- It is easier to have ten listings a month than to have ten buyers.

- Most top teams are listing-based.

<u>Leverage:</u> When you leverage the right listings, people, systems, technology, and database CRM, you can dramatically increase the number of homes you sell. The secret is to build a team that can run the system. Then, you stay in your unique ability of listing homes, negotiating contracts, removing conditions, and setting the vision for your business.

He also adds that your business should be prospecting-based and marketing-enhanced. This is why it is so important to learn about digital marketing, not only for people who do not know you already, but also retargeting back to your existing database. We need to keep our pipeline full of leads at all times. As I previously mentioned in chapter 1, you must learn how to market in the digital world, or partner with someone that already has this capability.

<u>Understand the business language of Real Estate:</u> Numbers speak. They tell you if you are on track to hit your goals. The numbers we need to track begin with the number of leads, the number of appointments, the number of contracts signed, the number of units sold, and the number of closed units. From these numbers, we can track how we are doing by benchmarking to the industry. Your local board or national body will publish results weekly and monthly. How are you doing compared to those numbers?

Learner	
Lie down	Double down
Did not learn anything during shutdown	Spent all their time learning
Already know everything	Always learning for more earning
No idea about market stats	Studies the market daily
No systems in business	Improving all systems daily
Hope for leads	Focus on leads, leverage, listings

Okay, so the third mindset is to become learning-based. Make sure that is the foundation for all of your 100-day sprints right now. This is the time you get to learn, so you will be positioned to earn!

Action steps:

1. The last six weeks were a time for you to learn in order to earn. Many of you are *zoomed out.*

2. Start moving from 50% virtual and 50% physical over the next thirty-100 days to 80% virtual and 20% physical by year-end.

3. Adopt the mindset that you see everything you have learned is preparation for greater learning. You are always trying to get better for the sake of getting better to grow your business.

4. Take one-two hours per day to improve all of your systems, tools, technology, presentations, scripts, and digital marketing.

5. Your business is prospecting based and marketing enhanced.

6. Understand that this business is about leads, leverage, and listings. Learn to track your numbers, and watch your money.

7. Look at every tool, model, and system you have and ask yourself what can you do today to make it easier, simpler, faster, and more enjoyable for my customer to do business with me?

4
GAME CHANGER

Create new value for others and reap the
advantages in the market place

THE FOURTH MINDSET we need to work on for our
Shutdown Slingshot 100-day sprint is how to become a game-
changer. A game-changer is someone who looks at the massive
shift the pandemic caused and utilizes that to create new value
for others and reap all of the advantages in the marketplace.

According to the dictionary, the definition of "game
changer" is: a person who is a visionary or a company that
alters its business strategy and conceives an entirely new
business plan. This type of company switches up and forms
a new business strategy to compete directly or indirectly with
competitors." (Investopedia.com)

There has never been a better opportunity for you than
right now! What I love about this is how we get to change

the game right now in the real estate industry. Being a game-changer does not mean switching to an entirely different game. It means utilizing the best of the proven models that exist right now in our industry and making small but meaningful adjustments to them.

Over the past ten years, we have had to endure numerous companies that have tried to disrupt our industry. According to the latest numbers from Statista, global investment in Proptech companies has grown from US $1 billion in 2012 to US $18 billion in 2018. That included companies like Zillow, Trulia, or Redfin, which utilizes search and big data, or iBuyer, a company that uses technology to make an offer on your home instantly using Offerpad or Opendoor. A lot of these people were trying to snatch the industry away from the agents. They seemed to think this was only a transactional business that could be commoditized. But most of the transactions we do are about 90-95% emotional, and the actual transaction and negotiating make up about 5-10% of the total time you spend with that individual.

Let us look at the best or worst mindsets to become a game-changer. The worst mindset around this is when you think your biggest growth and achievement are in the past. You are holding on to what you have because you do not want to lose it. This is where a lot of people live in our industry. I want them to stay there because the longer they feel that way and live with that fixed mindset, the more opportunities for the rest of us.

Let us look at what the opposite of that is, the growth mindset. The best mindset is believing everything you have done in your past is preparation for much greater growth, progress, and achievement. Reframe your thinking to, *I am grateful for everything that I learned in the past, and it is the foundation for my great learning and growth.*

You should be looking at the market right now and thinking, *How do we get to change this game?* Well, I think one of the best ways you can change the game is by simply making it faster, simpler, and easier for the consumer. This means that you have all the tools ready to do virtual tours, virtual open houses, virtual consultations, and offering *live* offer negotiations via Zoom. You could invite the other person to come in and present their offer. We no longer need to gather all the offers by email and present them to the seller. You could also create an environment for agents to have the opportunity to present their offer. On Zoom, you can control how long they come in for, how long they talk, and you can kick them out of the meeting whenever you want to.

What a great way to start thinking about how we can change this entire industry. What is the big opportunity for you right now? What game do you want to change? Where is the gap in the market that you could fill? How can you alter your business plan and direct it to the new opportunities in the marketplace?

The biggest opportunity is moving away from being a commodity agent, the type of agent who is trying to be everything to everyone. This agent often ends up not bringing much value to anyone. Many people enter the real estate business and run around to do a rental or a commercial listing, and they try to get a listing anywhere to survive. However, the biggest game changer right now is to create your niche market, which you could easily dominate in a couple of hours. All the information that you need right now to dominate one single niche market is at your fingertips—on the internet.

Here are three rules you have to think about how to pick a niche market:

It has to meet a unique need by providing a unique solution. So, your niche market is not first time buyers. It is first time buyers with a very specific need. It is not home sellers, but it is people selling because they are going through a divorce, so they are downsizing. Or, maybe it is helping investors to buy investment properties. The other rule for this is your niche market must speak to your prospects *hot buttons* by saying the right things.

The second rule is to complete a SWOT analysis. The SWOT analysis is a tool for you to identify the strengths, weaknesses, opportunities, and threats to be a game-changer. Being a game-changer means dominating one single target market. The easiest market to dominate is the one that comes most naturally to you, an area that you already have expertise in. Perhaps you came from another industry before getting into real estate. What skills did you bring with you?

The third rule is to ask yourself the game-changer question—what could you do to add so much value to a target market at such a reasonable price that you basically would have no competition? Then, get going before your competitor does! Go and create that as quickly as possible. Time stops for nobody, and the race is on to be a game-changer and disrupt your market.

Look at what markets are not being served right now. Where are the high-margin and low-competition markets? Consider what segments have changed when the market shifted. What segments did not change? For example, people get divorced in a good market and in a bad market. Look at your threats—what competitor beats you in the marketplace right now?

Four rules for entering a niche market: The first rule is that your niche market has to meet a unique need to the consumer by providing a unique solution to their selfish needs. So, we do not plan a general category such as first-time buyers. Instead, it is first-time buyers with a very specific need. It is not home sellers, but it is the people who are selling because they are going through a divorce or because they are downsizing. Or, it may be helping investors buy investment properties.

The second rule in creating a niche market is it must speak to your prospects' hot buttons by saying the right things *to them*. What is keeping them awake at night? What is their biggest fear? Then use those answers in your marketing to them.

The third rule is to enter a market that comes most naturally to you, where you already have expertise. You might have come from another industry before getting into real estate. What strengths did you bring with you? How can you maximize your existing strengths and then direct them to your target market?

I have found that most agents like working with people who are most like themselves. They have similar beliefs, values, and traits that make the real estate transaction fun and seamless. The challenge is when you are working with non-fit clients. The transaction becomes long, painful, and dreadful. The goal is to be working with people who you love to work with all the time. You must also look around and see what markets are being underserved right now. Where is the high margin, low competition market?

What segments will not change when a market shifts? What markets only change during a shift? During a recession, there is massive growth in the number of foreclosed homes, short-sales, or power of sales. Who is serving that market now? Is there an opportunity for you to direct all of your energies to that target market right now? People get divorced in a good market and in a bad market.

It is important to look at your threats from competitors. Where are they gaining market share? Do you want to compete against them or find a different opportunity?

The fourth rule for entering a niche market is to *dip your toe in first*. Test the market before committing a lot of time and effort. Start sharing your idea with people in your sphere of influence and listen to their feedback. Are you getting a sense of excitement from them or just a shrug? Try to do a mini seminar on the topic and see if anyone shows up online.

Your new game changer is going to be identifying one underserved niche market while everyone else is chasing the crumbs around right now. Our volumes dropped about 80%. It is going to be hyper competition for that 20%, and a lot of people are going to drop their fees or drop their commission to survive. Then, you will bypass that completely and enter the world of no competition niche markets.

Four reasons niche markets are so profitable:

1. People want to work with people who get them. And when you position yourself as a niche market specialist to solve someone's selfish need, you win their hearts, mind, and business.

2. People pay more for a specialist than a generalist. Throughout our adult lives, we get accustomed to paying more for specialist products goods and services. So, the public is already primed to pay more for a specialist than a generalist. This is why niche markets are so profitable. People are accustomed to paying more for a specialist in every area of their life. So, if you market yourself as this specialist, and you actually know that niche market better than anyone else, then getting paid a premium fee is never going to be a problem.

3. Become a highly visible celebrity specialist in your niche. You create this and position yourself as a specialist by writing blogs, making Youtube videos, Facebook pages, Instagram, or by doing podcasts. All of your social media resources line up to fit what your target

market prospect is looking for. This is the way to find the clients who are the perfect fit. You can then amplify this through paid social media advertising or grow organic through posts, seminars, and podcasts.

4. Your marketing expenses decrease dramatically. People start coming to you instead of you chasing them.

And it is just the magic of doing business in a low competition, high margin business.

Game Changer	
Lie down	Double down
Takes what they can get	Gets what they want
Takes the market	Adopt and create a market
Biggest growth in past	Biggest growth in the future
Trying to be everything to everyone	Is something to someone
Generalist	Specialist with Niche market

For additional insight, read my book, *The McQueenie Method-Own Your Niche, Own Your Market.* It is available as a free download at www.glennmcqueenie.com. Your new game changer is identifying one underserved niche market. While everyone else is chasing the crumbs (right now sales volumes dropped about 80%, and it is going to be hyper competition for that last 20% as a lot of people are going to drop their commission to survive), you get to bypass this completely and enter the *no competition* world of niche markets.

Action steps:

1. The disrupters are gone for now. Run fast and get your market before they come back.

2. The best mindset is that everything you have done in your past is preparation for much greater growth progress and achievement.

3. Move away from being a commodity agent, the type of agent who is trying to be everything to everyone.

4. The biggest game changer right now is to create your niche market.

5. The SWOT analysis is a tool for you to identify the strengths, the weaknesses, the opportunities, and the threats to be a game-changer.

6. Your niche market has to meet a unique need to the consumer by providing a unique solution to their selfish needs.

7. Line up to a market that comes most naturally to you and where you already have expertise.

8. What markets only change during a shift? Which stay the same?

9. Niche markets are very profitable.

5
ACHIEVER

Be a high achiever and get incredible results with a clear and focused mindset

BEING FOCUSED ON results is the fifth mindset that you are going to need to get out of the shutdown slingshot and rapidly grow your business over the next 100 days. We are actually going to be dealing with two complete waves during this pandemic. "The first is the Virus wave, or the pandemic wave. And the second wave is the Economic fallout as a result of the first wave." (Gene Rivers, Operating Principal at Keller Williams Panama City.)

I feel this could be even more brutal than the virus wave.

Gene Rivers adds, "A lot of research that we've been doing seems to point to that for every one month the economy is shut down during a pandemic, results in two to four months of a slower economic recovery."

So, the bigger game here is we do not really know how long the virus wave or pandemic wave will be. The longer it lasts, the longer it will take the economy to recover. So, for every one month of the virus, it is two to four months of recovery. So, if this continues for two or three months, we could be easily looking at anywhere from six to twelve to fourteen months to get ourselves back to where we used to be. It could also be more logarithmic. That is, for every month you are shutdown, your recovery time will be multiplied. i.e. A three-month lockdown will be a sixteen to twenty-four month recovery time.

How do you win the game amidst all of this uncertainty? Well, the number one thing you need to do is move very fast from shut down, like all your competition, to double down. And when I talk about double down, I am talking about if you want to make the same amount of money you made last year, you are going to have to work twice as hard, which means you are going to have to go on twice as many appointments and generate twice as many leads and generally work twice as much as you did before.

Now is your time to grab market share! Smart agents agree that the greatest opportunity of a shifted market is to gain market share. A shift in the market forces agents to get back to the basics or get out of the market. The basics are lead generation, booking appointments, lead conversion, taking listing/buying contracts, negotiating offers, removing the conditions, and get the transaction to closing. This is your top 20%, nothing else matters. Those agents who adjust their tactics to meet the demands of the market place will manage to hold their transaction count and volumes steady and may even gain market share as the total market declines.

The question is how we schedule our time every day. If we have to double up on the amount of time we spend lead generating and for appointments, I would suggest right now that your mornings should be all lead generation. This starts by doing at least three to four hours every single morning. Book all your appointments for the afternoon via Zoom, whether it be buyer consultations or listing consultations. I think the goal for you is to have one listing consultation and one buyer consultation every single day.

The later part of the day is when you can be working on any of the systems or tools or technologies. That will make your business faster, simpler, and easier to run. So, if we can spend half of our day lead generating and half on appointments, you really are constructing what we call the perfect day.

So, what is the mindset required for you to be focused on results? The worst mindset that you could possibly have is to do the minimum amount of time and effort, since that is what you get paid for, regardless of the final result. This is not the mindset of a warrior, but it is more a mindset of an employee.

The opposite of this is the growth mindset. You see that everything you did in the past is preparation for much greater growth and progress. The growth mindset that you should be striving for is that you are focused on accomplishing your result regardless of the time and effort that is required. That is the mindset of a productivity warrior. It has got to get done. I set my goal, and I am going to stick to it regardless of how much time it takes to get the result that I need.

The next step in having a *focused on results* mindset is making the decision of how you are going to fit all of this into your schedule. Well, that begins with asking yourself what you need to do more of? What do you need to stop doing?

- Does my schedule line up with my goals?

- Could I be more diligent about prospecting?

- Have I tried other (and newer) sources for leads?

- Can I recite my scripts for every objection that buyers or sellers may throw at me?

- Is my messaging through marketing and prospecting clear?

- Is my unique selling proposition clear, and does it reflect what my customers expect and want from me?

You know, we all have the same number of hours in the day. Yet high achievers will be able to get incredible results compared to lower achievers because they are very clear on what they need to be focused on. So, the question is what do you need to stop doing right now? And what do you need to start doing so that your focused result mindset will line up with the goals you have set for yourself?

The simplest way I found to set goals is to start with this very simple model called the 1-3-5. The 1 stands for your annual income goal, or it could be the transaction goal. How many homes do you sell? The 3 stands for the three strategies you need to do to support your annual goal. One of those strategies would be scheduling and completing your lead generation, every single day. The second would be converting all of your appointments or as many appointments as you can to written sales contracts. Your third would be selling as many houses as you need to with buyers and sellers, whether it is per week or per month to support the annual goal.

So, if you are doing all the lead generation and you are getting all the contracts, then you are closing on all those contracts. You can pretty well predict that you are going to hit your annual goal or your *one thing*. And then underneath each one of those three strategies, there is what we call 5 priorities. So, for lead generation, you would write down what the five priorities you need to do to make sure you have enough time in your schedule.

To lead generate every day, you will have to focus on getting proper sleep, proper exercise, and having the right morning rituals. Get rid of your old habits of not having a daily schedule, and create a new habit of following one. Put lead generation, appointments, and conversion time in your calendar, and then focus on executing it every day. You will be able to stay on track, and you will be able to focus on your results and have the mindset of a high achiever. Then, you get to make every goal or dream you have come true. It all starts with being focused on results.

The final step of focusing on results you will make is to go through all of your active clients right now and put them into three categories. Are they yes, no, or maybe? Ask them if they are seriously thinking about buying or selling a home in the next thirty-ninety days. If they are serious, then start pouring all of your efforts into them. 80% of your focus and efforts are spent on the people who want to do something now.

If they are not serious, then ask them when they would like you to follow-up and check in again. If they say in five months because they think the economy will be a little bit more stable, make a note to follow up. Look at this as a gift because they told you already that they are not going to do anything, so you do not have to focus any more time on them right now.

The biggest breakthrough you will get is by pressuring your maybes into making a decision of yes or no.

I have seen so many agents have terrible quarters because they worked with so many people who were only *maybe* going to buy a home or *maybe* going to sell a home, and they never ended up doing anything for the entire ninety days or six months. All of a sudden, the agent is working with ten to twelve *maybes* and putting in all the time without producing anything.

This is the time to force your maybes to make a decision. They either get realistic right now or decide that they are going to buy or sell in the next thirty days, or if they are not, do not let them take up any more room in your mind right now.

Shifted markets challenge you to reflect on your past and current practices. It challenges you to return to basics. Being focused on results means spending 80% of your time on your key activities. As a reminder, the key activities are lead generation, booking appointments, lead conversion, taking listing/buying contracts, negotiating offers, removing the conditions, and get the transaction to closing. This is your top 20%, nothing else matters.

Focus all of your efforts on mastering the four things that you need to be successful:

1. Lead generate: find the lead generation model that best suits your natural behavioral style. Understand that marketing of the future will be 90% digital, 10% physical.

2. Master your people skills: people like to work with people that they like, trust, and respect. Self-mastery is the key to attracting great clients.

3. Product knowledge: know the product in your marketplace, and learn everything you can about spotting structural deficiencies in homes and prices for replacement costs of all of the major structural, heating, electrical, windows, foundation, roofing, and also typical renovation costs for kitchens, bathrooms, flooring, and additions.

4. Be a master of negotiation, and know all of the required contract clauses for all types of properties you want to specialize in. For example: multiplexes, triplexes, stores with apartments, farms, rural properties, and condominiums.

Let's examine what top agents do:

1. They specialize in either only one geographic area or in one type of home (i.e. Luxury, etc.).

2. They dominate their market.

3. They spend more money per client on marketing than on anything else. The more you spend to acquire a client, the more power you have in your marketplace.

4. They send the right message at the right time to people who are receptive to hearing it.

5. People who like to go fishing know that different bait and lures target different fish. Top teams send the right lure to the right people.

6. They do not want to be everything to everyone.

7. They generally charge a premium price and understand that price is just a function of value. Show a bigger value, and charge a higher price.

8. Mental toughness: They can bounce back.

9. Action-oriented: They can seize opportunities and combine them with energy, desire, and drive.

10. Client oriented: They constantly strive to exceed their client's expectations and act as a consultant instead of a salesperson.

11. They know the business, and they master negotiating, financing, human nature, people skills, and they know the market.

12. Execute the fundamentals of a listing consultation. They build a rapport, adjust to the seller, deal with questions, and get them to sign listing agreements.

<u>Spend time in your database:</u> Keep a list of warm leads that should be kept warm with consistent communication.

1. Check in first and see how they are doing. Ask this simple question—How are you holding up? Be respectful and aware. Do not lead with real estate, but dive in if they bring it up.

2. Have ten conversations per day.

3. Dive into your active prospect bucket. Spend time every single day in your active prospect bucket trying to transition them from active prospects into current clients.

4. Serve your clients, and always air on the side of under-promising and over-delivering.

5. Give: This means you need to disseminate helpful information to your sphere/database through emails, blog posts, social media posts, and/or YouTube videos.

6. Ask/Receive for referrals: Have winning referral conversations.

7. Do not fight with customers who are not the right fit for you. Just find better playmates.

Achiever	
Lie down	Double down
Not focused on results	Completely results focused
No Business Plan	Follows a business plan
No real schedule	Plans out key activities and schedule
Spends time in bottom 80%	Spends most of their time in top 20%
Hates accountability	Loves deadlines and accountability

These are the tools that make you focus on results. Now is your time to grab market share! Smart agents agree that the greatest opportunity of a shifted market is to gain market share if you seize the opportunity.

Action steps:

1. I am focused on achieving my results regardless of the amount of time and effort that is required. It has to get done!

2. Align your schedule to your goals. We all have the same amount of time in a day, but high achievers will win because their priorities and focus are clear.

3. Move very fast from shut down to double down.

4. Start by doing at least three to four hours of lead generation every single morning. Book all your appointments for the afternoon via Zoom whether it be buyer consultations or listing consultations.

5. The later part of the day you can be working on any of the systems or tools or technologies. That is going to be making your business faster, simpler, and easier to run.

6. Do a 1-3-5 today: One annual goal, three strategies to hit the goal, five priorities for each of your three strategies.

7. Model what top agents do.

8. Spend a lot of time in your database. This is where the easier business comes from.

6
PLAYER

Improve your inner game constantly to see your biggest growth results

Every game (of tennis) is composed of two parts, an outer game, and an inner game . . . It is the thesis of this book that neither mastery nor satisfaction can be found in the playing of any game without giving some attention to the relatively neglected skills of the inner game. This is the game that takes place in the mind of the player, and it is played against such obstacles as lapses in concentration, nervousness, self-doubt, and self-condemnation. In short, it is played to overcome all habits of mind which inhibit excellence in performance. . . . Victories in the inner game may provide no additions to the trophy case, but they bring valuable rewards which are more permanent and which can contribute significantly to one's success, off the court as well as on.

—W. Timothy Gallwey, *The Inner Game of Tennis*

THERE ARE TWO choices when it comes to working and developing your inner game. One could be that nobody understands you, so you feel increasingly resentful and intimidated by other people's advantages or successes. The more growth-oriented mindset around this begins when you realize that your biggest growth will occur when you constantly improve your inner game. Your mastery of your inner game works to serve the mastery of your outer game.

Something that I have learned through being in the real estate business for a long time is that you are really in the mindset-attracting business. When you work with people who have similar values, mindsets, and beliefs, you get a friction-free, fun, real estate transaction. High production and cash confidence raise your vibrational energy and attract more high-energy business to you. This is why deals *fall* on our lap when you are on a roll.

Be a person of high integrity, strong character, and high morals. Have a great work ethic and be learning-based. Attend all the training you can. Be kind and treat your colleagues with respect. Have a life mission, and follow a business-plan. Discover your big *why,* and follow the platinum rule, which is to *treat other people how they would like to be treated.*

When we work with clients who have opposing values, beliefs, and perspectives, every transaction becomes very difficult.

However, it is hard to attract others when you do not feel good about yourself. The irony in this is you will feel good about yourself when you are helping others. When you are spending too much time in your head, you will likely end up in a negative state. However, it is almost impossible to be in a negative state when you are serving others. When others show you gratitude for the service that you provided, it is hard to feel bad about yourself.

Your inner game generates this confidence for your outer game. People are attracted to confident people. Consider this: what is the one thing you could do today to generate the biggest boost in your confidence? Having the right mindset becomes the greatest boost to your confidence. If your mindset is fear right now, you will attract fearful buyers and sellers and vice versa.

I have learned that great agents, despite the difficult events or setbacks they encounter, can respond in a fantastic way and succeed at a high level. They do this by being alert, curious, responsive, and most importantly, by being responsible for everything that happens to them. The bottom line is that 50% of your life is luck, either good or bad, and it is not what happens to you or your clients. It is how you respond.

It is time to minimize the level of fear you are having and more importantly, the level of fear that your clients are experiencing. Fear is a gift. The reason you exist today is because one of your ancestors did not get eaten by a lion or a tiger. They had to be aware of their surroundings and stay alive with a minimum amount of fear. Human beings make their best decisions when they have low levels of fear and their worst decisions when they are in panic mode. Your goal is to be the one who constantly lowers the level of your customer's fear.

Player	
Lie down	Double down
Nobody gets me	I have to work on my inner game
Focused on self	Improves outer game to focus on others
Similar value add as other agents	Constantly increases value to customers
Spends no time on their thinking	Is always thinking about their thinking
Inner focused and isolated	Outer focused and connected

Here are some action steps for you to follow:

1. Your biggest growth will occur when you constantly improve your inner game. Your mastery of your inner game works to serve the mastery of your outer game.

2. The first thing anyone buys into is a relationship. Therefore, now is the time to call and book appointments with every client you are working with and check in on how they are doing. You have two types of clients, passive and active. The active clients are everyone who you know who are thinking about buying or selling a home in the next thirty to ninety days. The passive clients are your sphere of influence, past clients, and referrals. Deepen your relationship one client at a time because deep relationships inspire confidence. Show me a person who has a lot of deep, great relationships, and I will show you a very confident person.

3. Increase your value through your leadership by giving them the gift of perspective. Tell them that we have just gotten through the toughest part of the market, and inventories will continue to rise throughout the summer and into the fall, and that every buyer you have ever worked with felt the same way they do right now. There has never been a buyer I have worked with who I have not been able to find a home. You should tell your buyers (and sellers) the same thing. A house will come, and they will get great money from their home, because that is what always happens. Leadership and value provide confidence by giving your clients the proper perspective.

4. The next step is to change your game and increase the level of value and contribution you bring to your clients. Successful agents go first and give as much value upfront before they ever expect anything in return. Low producing agents operate from massive scarcity and will never provide any value until a customer signs a buyer representation agreement or they are assured that at any minute, their effort will be compensated. Scarcity attracts scarcity; abundance attracts abundance. Therefore, your current mindset matters, always bringing more value to your clients.

5. Have a life mission and follow a business-plan. Discover your big *why*.

6. If you want to make even more money, you must first increase your level of thinking.

7. Your current level of thinking represents where you are today, but if you want to grow your business and double your income, you need to change the level of your thinking. So why not start now?

8. The final step to mastering your inner game mindset and understanding that your biggest growth occurs when you improve your inner game (because it gets reflected in the outer game) is to ask yourself this one question. Do I want to come out of this storm stronger or weaker than I am right now? If it is stronger, it is time to start internally focusing now and working on getting that inner game to the optimum level. It is about staying in your strengths and not spending any more time on your weaknesses. Focus on your strengths and hire out your weaknesses. When you spend 80% of your time doing what you love to do, you build a great real estate business. You also grow your inner game, which grows your outer game.

While we master the inner game, we cannot let any clutter get in our way. We have to achieve incredible clarity and confidence and work with people who really want to work with us and who have to do something, anything. As you continue to work on your inner game, your outer game will continue to grow, and you will build an amazing real estate empire!

7
GROWER

Win the game as you sprint past the competition

DRIVEN TO GROW is about having a growth mindset as opposed to having a fixed mindset. When you have a growth mindset, you have a deep-down drive and belief that you can control growing your knowledge, attitude, skills, and habits. It is a belief that you can create a bigger and brighter future for yourself and others. You really believe that your greatest satisfaction comes from increasing capabilities and results in every area of your life.

A fixed mindset, on the other hand, says you almost have to accept your lot in life. You have to take what life gave you. *I'll never be a great singer. I'll never be a great dancer. I can't dance.* I believe that in this hundred-day sprint, as we come out of the virus pandemic and get back into the real estate business, we have to have the mindset of growing as quickly as possible.

There has never been a time in my thirty-one years of real estate when the market had such a dramatic shift. This is going to go down in history as the biggest transfer of wealth from one group of individuals who have it to a new set of entrepreneurs who are about to come and get it. The old game is gone, and we are entering the new game right now. I remember the 2008/2009 shift. Some people who were number one faded right away, while others who were number three, four, five, or six suddenly started moving up into three, two, and one. This is your biggest opportunity market right now. And my wish for you is that you believe it and go out and grab it. Take the opportunity that has been given to you. Because if you do not, someone else will!

There are some great areas to focus on to become an even bigger growth mindset warrior.

1. You start to view every challenge as an opportunity. It gives you an unending ability to look at every challenge and ask, *How can I do this better?*

2. You adopt a growth mindset about failure. Instead of thinking about failure as a negative thing, what if you believed that all failing was future learning? Failing forward becomes learning forward.

3. Every time you reach a new goal, you should pause, be happy, feel gratitude about it, and get ready to set an even bigger goal. It is the fuel that keeps you going and keeps life exciting.

4. Be resilient, and do not give up. Other people gave up because it got too hard or too difficult. You powered through it because you actually used that resistance as a way to push your way forward and hit a new goal.

5. Being driven to grow becomes the new necessity. The economic loss has only started to be analyzed. Nobody knows how many jobs will return to the marketplace. We have no idea if prices will go up or down. We do not know if we are in a *v-shaped recovery*, a *w-shaped* (second viral wave returns), or a *u-shaped* (economy drops and takes a long time to recover). Each one of these recoveries will require different tools and strategies. The goal now is to be creative. Act fast to the ever-changing market, and get ready to gain your unfair share of the market.

6. What are three things that you have been procrastinating about completing? Your database? CRM program? Facebook Ads? Calling past clients? We all have three things if we take the time to complete them, they would propel your business forward. Your business would grow at least 50% if you just got them done and installed in your business.

7. Who on your team or allied network could you replace? Who could you partner with and grow your business (and theirs) exponentially? Is your current environment supporting your next level of growth or holding you back?

8. To double the size of your business, you do not need to double the amount of time you spend in it. There is no correlation between hours spent in your business and your income. I know some agents who make a lot of money and work half of the year. I also know agents that work seven days a week, fifteen hours a day, and barely make over $60,000.

9. Your skills are your security, not your money. Reading a book is like going to exercise. You do not go to the gym once and expect to be in shape.

10. It is all about your commitment to the task over time. It is not about more knowing. It is about more doing! Most people only go into action when they are losing something instead of being motivated for the gain. Growth warriors grow for the sake of growing.

11. You know, in the next year or two, the real estate industry is really going to challenge you. You might want to even look back and know you yearned for the good old days, but I am telling you good news. Adopting a growth mindset and going after it will be your biggest breakthrough.

Eight ways to create more value for your client and sphere:

1. Establishing (or re-establishing) long-term growth relationships with your clients and customers, who become your greatest sales force.

2. Differentiate yourself from all of your would-be competitors in the industry in ways that are appealing, impactful, and permanent.

3. Attract high-quality team members to your team of allied service providers. Rank your current relationships, and decide on which ones that you want to upgrade.

4. Plan to take a vacation every six weeks for at least ten days to ensure that you are at your highest self when you meet your customers.

5. Never settle: Always be a pusher for better relationships with your team and customers.

6. Perceived value equals the amount of money you can charge for your services. Always increase your value

and perceived value so that you become irreplaceable to your clients and customers.

7. For your clients, it is not the deal that you got them. It is the deal that they think they just got. It is this perception that will govern your future relationship.

Your greatest satisfaction will come from continually measuring your increased capabilities and results in every area of your business. Being driven to grow is your game-changer. While everybody tries to hang on to what they have, you sprint past them and win the game.

Grower	
Lie down	Double down
Take what life gives you	Always be growing for the sake of growing
Everything is a challenge	Every challenge is an opportunity
No resilience	Extremely resilient to every setback
Money is my security	Skills are your security
Knows a lot about everything	Learns and knows for sake of doing

Action steps:

1. You really believe that your greatest satisfaction comes from increasing capabilities and results in every area of your life.

2. There has never been a time in my thirty-one years of real estate when the market had such a dramatic

shift. This is going to go down in history as the biggest transfer of wealth from one group of individuals who have it to a new set of entrepreneurs who are just about to come and get it.

3. Be resilient; do not give up.

4. What are three things that you have been procrastinating about completing? Just do them now, and they will be your greatest leap forward.

5. Never settle. Always be a pusher for better relationships with your team and customers.

6. It is all about your commitment to the task over time. It is not about more knowing. It is about more doing.

7. Perceived value equals the amount of money you can charge for your services. Always be increasing you value and perceived value so that you become irreplaceable to your clients and customers.

8
TESTER

Consider the marketplace as your creative partner for developing new methods, concepts, products and services.

THIS IS YOUR opportunity to try some really new ideas and get the feedback from the marketplace. What I have noticed is that when the market shifts, the innovators are the people who win the game. Success is never linear. What an innovator attempts does not always work. I find they just fail their way forward. And this is the time for us to really get out there and be brave and test as many new creative ideas as we can come up with. The best mindset around this is to try new concepts, and consider the marketplace your creative partner for developing new concepts, methods, products, and services. You cherish their feedback, and then adjust your offerings.

The alternative is to never try and never test a new product and service and get feedback from the marketplace. Even worse is to ignore other people's feedback regarding your performance and their results.

So, before we go into testing, we should actually base this on a foundation of facts. The facts that I would love to base a lot of my creativity on is an annual Home Buyer/Seller survey, done by the National Association of Realtors. It is called the NAR home Buyer/Seller profile. They survey thousands of buyers and sellers in the United States. And then they publish their results every year. See below for the highlights from 2019.

NAR Home Buyer/Seller Profile 2019

Results of Survey from Buyers

- 89% of buyers recently purchased their home through a real estate agent. Only 5% purchased directly from a builder or builder's agent.

- Having an agent to help them find the right home was what buyers wanted most when choosing an agent at 52%.

- 41% of buyers used an agent who was referred to them by a friend, neighbor, or relative.

- 75% of buyers interviewed only one real estate agent during their home search.

- 90% of buyers would use their agent again or recommend their agent to others.

Home Sellers and Their Selling Experience

- 89% of home sellers worked with a real estate agent to sell their home.

- 66% of sellers were very satisfied with the selling process. Many were satisfied, and very few were unsatisfied.

- 66% of sellers found their agent through a referral from a friend, neighbor, or relative. Or, they used an agent they had worked with before to buy or sell a home.

- 75% of sellers contacted only one agent before finding the right agent they worked with to sell their home.

- The typical seller has recommended their agent once since selling their home. 36% of sellers recommended their agent three or more times since selling their home.

- Only eight of recent home sales were FSBO sales again this year. This remains near the lowest share recorded since this report started in 1981.

What sellers really want from you: "Sellers placed high priority on the following five tasks: market the home to potential buyers (21%), sell the home within a specific timeframe (20%), price the home competitively (19%), help fix the home to sell for more (16%), and find a buyer for the home (13%)."

If we build all of our systems to support the five key needs of sellers, we have solved 89% of their priorities.

1. **Market the home to potential buyers (21%).** Utilize Virtual tours and 3D tours. Have the seller walk through the house and film each room individually, so you can edit it all together and do a voice-over. Hold virtual showing times and virtual open houses. Note:

most condo buildings do not allow public open houses, but now you can do virtual open houses! 98% of the marketing of the property will be price and condition.

2. **Sell the home within a specific timeframe (20%).** Be the local economist of choice and show days on market, inventory, percentage of asking, highest turn-over price ranges.

3. **Price the home competitively (19%).** Do Virtual CMA's via Zoom with walk-through and virtual showings of competing homes. Map competing homes, recent solds, and expireds.

4. **Help fix the home to sell for more (16%)**. Do Virtual staging. Provide Digital Home Inspection Report.

5. **Find a buyer for the home (13%). Facebook targeted ad's Google ad's Instagram marketing**. Record your video walk through but keep yourself out of it. Allow other Realtor's to share your tours with their buyers. Make it easy to accept offers digitally and make deposits via wire transfer.

What Buyers Want from Agents and Benefits Provided

The most important characteristic to recent buyers when looking for a real estate agent was to find someone who could help them find the right home to purchase (52%). Buyers were also looking for someone who could help them negotiate the terms of sale (12%) and help with price negotiations (11%). Help with the paperwork was 8%. If we satisfy these five priorities, we have satisfied 89% of their needs and wants.

1. **Finding someone who could help them find the right home to purchase (52%).** Create virtual seminars, virtual buyer consultations, and virtual home buying guides. Create Youtube videos that walk them through the entire home buying journey, and position yourself as the helpful expert. Create virtual showing Zooms where you line up six properties for them to tour.

2. **Help them negotiate the terms of sale (12%). Help with price negotiations (11%).** All of the negotiations can be done virtually. Produce guides on how to effectively negotiate the best price for a home and offer them free by email or text. Advise them on how to win on multiple offer situation. Do a seminar, podcast, or blog on negotiating or winning in multiple offers.

3. **Help with paperwork 8%.** Produce sample offers with most popular terms and conditions already inserted.

4. **Determine what comparable homes were selling for 6%.** You could create virtual market analysis and review recent sales with buyer, complete with mapping.

What can you create and become a game-changer? What new systems could you add to the list that will give you a massive advantage over the competition? What can you test right now? What could you improve on right now to make the whole transaction faster, simpler, easier, and more lucrative for you?

Tester	
Lie down	Double down
Already knows what people want	Finds out what they want and delivers
Focuses on selfish needs	Focuses on needs of others
Hates change	Loves change
Hates feedback	Loves feedback
Loses market share	Gains market share

Action steps:

1. Every new innovation you create is first measured against the facts of what consumers really want.

2. Every tool is designed to solve the selfish needs of what buyers and sellers really want from you.

3. Every innovation is rolled out at the *minimum effective dose* stage, to test in the marketplace.

4. You cherish their feedback, and then adjust your offerings.

5. Build all of our systems to support the five key needs of sellers mentioned in this chapter. If you do, you have solved 89% of their priorities.

In times of great change comes great opportunity. This book focused on the eight winning mindsets you need to survive and thrive in the post-pandemic world:

1. Digitize everything you do, and act virtually.

2. Be disruptive. Be really disruptive.

3. Be learning-based and open to the opportunity.

4. Be a game-changer.

5. Focus on results—it's progress, not perfection.

6. Always be working on your inner game to have the best outer game.

7. Be driven to grow, and have a growth mindset.

8. Constantly test the market. Get feedback from the market and adapt.

While others shut down, you will double down. I believe the work you do now will set you up for the final two quarters of 2020 and the rest of your real estate career. It is your turn to implement these mindsets and action steps into your business.

As I mentioned at the beginning, the agents who use this book over the next 100 days (starting first within the next thirty days) will take a massive market share from those who have shut down and cease to work during the pandemic. While some agents shut down, I want you to double-down. Doubling-down will increase business and allow you to avoid database shrinkage through loss to your competition, and it will prepare you for a quick recovery in the post-pandemic world. The seeds we sow now will be harvested in the fall.

The next 100 days will pass no matter what action you take (or you don't take), but you have the opportunity to sprint into the future and set your business up to rebound to even greater heights. Follow the *Shutdown Slingshot*, and take massive market share from those agents in shut down or who are just unwilling to change.

Be disruptive, and understand that this new game will be the biggest transfer of market share in your career.

If this book has inspired you to get ahead of the competition, there are three steps you can take today.

1. Visit glennmcqueenie.com to download a copy of my niche market book, *The McQueenie Method,* for free. It gives a more detailed look at discovering your niche market.

2. While you are there, visit the download page and get a copy of the 1-3-5 business planning tool. Also, take part in my Scorecard to assess where your current thinking is today.

3. Join me for some great group coaching at the *winning mindset masterclass,* or private one-on-one coaching with the "Slingshot Coaching" program.

   I know that every disruption has winners who take action and can come out disproportionately ahead of the competition. If you want to talk more about the tools we have to boost your business, shoot me an email to glennmcqueenie@gmail.com, and we will take it from there.

BIBLIOGRAPHY

Investopedia. "Game Changer." https://www.investopedia.com/terms/g/game-changer.asp/ (accessed April 30, 2020)

Simmons, Quintin. "Families Using Creativity When Buying, Selling Homes: 2019 Buyer, Seller Survey." Nar.realtor. https://www.nar.realtor/newsroom/families-using-creativity-when-buying-selling-homes-2019-buyer-and-seller-survey, (accessed May 1, 2019)

ABOUT THE AUTHOR

Glenn is the CEO of three real estate franchise offices in Ontario, with over 550 amazing agents. He is the CEO of Referred Advance Inc. and Touch 33 Marketing Ltd. He is a licensed realtor for over thirty-one years and a Co-Founder, Investor/Regional Training Director for KW Romania.

Glenn started with a small independent company in 1989, then spent twelve years at Re/Max before opening the first Keller Williams office in Southern Ontario. These offices have grown to over 550 Realtors and forty Employees in four offices. He is the author of *Double Your Income- The simple way for Real Estate Agents to make more money, in less time, working with the clients they really love*, and *The McQueenie Method—Own Your Niche, Own Your Market*. Member of Strategic Coach (Dan Sullivan) Toronto, previously with Genius Network (Joe Polish) Arizona. 2015 Award winning Quantum Leap for Youth Instructor.

Glenn is also a mentor and coach to top agents throughout North America and also teaches internationally.

Glenn is committed to raising the bar in real estate by creating a new generation of realtors who are learning-based, serve their clients at the highest levels, and with a culture of high integrity, leadership, and character. He believes in coming from contribution, growing for the sake of growing, and inspiring a whole new generation of Entrepreneurs.

Glenn lives in Toronto, Ontario, with his spouse, Janet, children, Gavin and Erin, and an overly friendly Golden Retriever, named Marlowe.

THE
SHUTDOWN SLINGSHOT
SCORECARD

Crush the Competition!

What's your current thinking about the market? Use *The Shutdown Slingshot Scorecard* to find out! Once you know your score, you can learn how to shift your current thinking and business into one that is even more efficient and profitable.

tinyurl.com/shutdownslingshot

MASTERCLASS

Experience the
Winning Mindset Masterclass!

| DISRUPTER | GAME CHANGER | PLAYER | TESTER |
| DIGITIZER | LEARNER | ACHIEVER | GROWER |

Success in real estate is 90% mindset and 10% talent.

Do you know what action steps you need to take?

Glenn helps you go deeper, and master the 8 winning mindsets for thriving in a post-pandemic economy and boosting long-term profitability.

ShutdownSlingshotBook.com

COACHING

Private one-on-one
"Slingshot Coaching" with me!

» **Leverage the 8 winning mindsets needed for increased productivity and profitability**

» **Get the mentorship you need to fast-track your business**

» **Learn the systems that can increase your capabilities and enhance your success**

ShutdownSlingshotBook.com

Manufactured by Amazon.ca
Bolton, ON

13600923R00048